Crafting with Stickers

Crafting with Stickers

Carol Scheffler

what a friend!

Sterling Publishing Co., Inc. New York
A Sterling/Chapelle Book

Chapelle, Ltd.:
  Jo Packham
  Sara Toliver
  Cindy Stoeckl

  Editor: Jennifer Luman
  Art Director: Karla Haberstich
  Graphic Illustrator: Kim Taylor
  Copy Editor: Marilyn Goff

  Staff: Kelly Ashkettle, Areta Bingham,
Donna Chambers, Emily Frandsen, Lana Hall, Mackenzie Johnson,
Susan Jorgensen, Melissa Maynard, Barbara Milburn, Lecia Monsen,
Suzy Skadburg, Linda Vendetti, Desirée Wybrow

If you have any questions or comments,
please contact:
Chapelle, Ltd., Inc., P.O. Box 9252, Ogden, UT 84409
  (801) 621-2777 • (801) 621-2788 Fax
  e-mail: chapelle@chapelleltd.com
  web site: www.chapelleltd.com

Library of Congress Cataloging-in-Publication Data

Scheffler, Carol
    Crafting with stickers / Carol Scheffler.
      p. cm.
    "A Sterling/Chapelle Book."
    Includes Index.
      ISBN 1-4027-0723-1
      1. Paper work. 2. Stickers. I. Title.
TT870 .S2897 2003
745.5--dc22

                           2003019926

10 9 8 7 6 5 4 3 2 1

Published by Sterling Publishing Co., Inc.
387 Park Avenue South, New York, NY 10016
©2004 by Carol Scheffler
Distributed in Canada by Sterling Publishing
c/o Canadian Manda Group, One Atlantic Avenue, Suite 105
Toronto, Ontario, Canada M6K 3E7
Distributed in Great Britain by Chrysalis Books
64 Brewery Road, London N7 9NT, England
Distributed in Australia by Capricorn Link (Australia) Pty. Ltd.
P. O. Box 704, Windsor, NSW 2756, Australia
Printed and Bound in China
All Rights Reserved

Sterling ISBN 1-4027-0723-1

Introduction

What is a sticker? Silly question, right? After all, everyone knows what a sticker is. It is a small piece of glossy paper that is printed with an image, usually something cute. It has an adhesive back that is exposed once it is pulled away from its release paper.

That description of a sticker would have been accurate several years ago. However, if you haven't wandered into your local craft or scrapbooking store lately, you may be surprised to see what stickers look like today. Stickers are now made of metal, plastic, embroidered fabric, and, yes, paper. And stickers are not necessarily flat anymore. In fact, many stickers you will see in this book include dimension through the addition of paper layering, buttons, metal, wire, feathers, and jewels.

The paper that stickers are printed on these days isn't necessarily glossy either. Stickers are printed on vellum, holographic and glitter papers, cardstock, and handmade papers. Stickers come in all sizes—from tiny to quite large. Ever seen a 12"-long sticker?!

Several years ago, we decorated envelopes with stickers, or created motivational chore charts for our children. However, with the wide range of beautiful stickers available today, creating sophisticated sticker art is limited only by our imaginations.

I've gathered some of my favorite new stickers from the most inventive sticker companies. I will show you a myriad of sticker techniques to help you achieve really great looking projects. I will also show you tricks for using stickers on a wide range of surfaces beyond paper. The beauty of these projects is that they almost all fall into the category of "quick and easy." After all, stickers were created to be easy, time-saving additions to your creative projects.

I will begin by showing you how to make your own stickers so that you can completely customize your project to suit your vision.

So, throw away any old, limited notions of what you thought you could do with stickers. I want to open your eyes to the exciting possibilities of *Crafting with Stickers.*

Carol Scheffler

Table of Contents

General Instructions

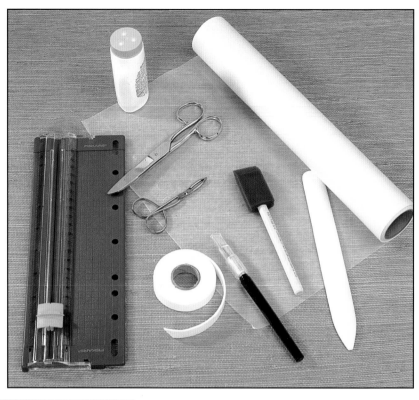

Tools Most of the tools you will need to incorporate stickers into your creative projects are things you probably already own. Here are some useful tools you will need for creating various effects: baking or baby powder, a burnishing tool (like a bone folder or the edge of a credit card), craft knife, craft scissors, foam brush, foam tape, small paper cutter, tweezers, waxed paper.

Organization There are two approaches to organizing a sticker collection; both are useful in certain circumstances. For each approach, there are a number of organization options.

Organizing by manufacturer—Many companies that make stickers often make matching paper. Designing a page with the paper and matching stickers is a timesaving approach to scrapbooking and card making that produces beautiful results. Storing these coordinated elements together in a large plastic sleeve makes sense.

Organizing by theme—Some companies concentrate more on manufacturing stickers. They offer them in a wide range of themes and designs. Organizing these stickers by theme makes them easiest to access and use.

Storage

Store your images relating to a certain theme together. For example, store all birthday images such as confetti, presents, cakes, candles, blowers, words, etc., together so that they are handy to grab for a quick card or scrapbook page.

There are several useful options for storing themed stickers. If you have a very small sticker collection (and, trust me, it won't stay small for long!), a coupon organizer can work well to get you started.

As your collection grows, an expandable file folder is an inexpensive option. For a large sticker collection, consider a notebook filled with plastic sleeves divided into individual sections.

Several companies make zippered cloth notebooks filled with pages made specifically for sticker storage. Photograph storage boxes such as those pictured below are a great idea if your stickers are stored on shelves.

How to make your own stickers

There are a number of ways to make your own stickers, allowing you to completely customize the look you are trying to achieve. I will introduce you to some new tools you may not be familiar with that will help you create your own stickers; but keep your eyes open in your local craft or paper-arts store for new products as well. Manufacturers are always coming out with materials to challenge crafter's imaginations.

Autumn Leaf Sticker

The Xyron® machine allows you to add a thin, even layer of permanent or temporary adhesive to the back of any relatively flat surface. In this card, an autumn leaf has been run through the hand-cranked machine and permanent adhesive has been applied, transforming the leaf into a sticker. Consider doing the same to other ephemera such as a ticket stub, feather, dried flower, length of ribbon, an antique valentine, or perfume label.

Adhesive-backed Bumblebee Sticker

Adhesive-backed paper is available in a variety of colors, patterns, and vellum. Dee Gruenig from Posh Impressions championed the use of creating stickers with white adhesive-backed paper and rubber stamps. She created the card below using Posh Impression's bumblebee and frame stamps. Photocopying clip art, magazine cutouts, original art, or photographs onto white adhesive-backed paper is also an option.

Notice how the framed bee and word rectangles appear to be floating above the card. This effect is achieved by shadowing the featured elements with a gray water-based marker. Make certain that the shadow is applied before the elements are adhered onto the card so that they can overlap the shadow, supporting the illusion even further.

Die-cut Star Stickers

Making die-cuts from adhesive-backed shelving paper or sticker paper is a simple way to create many stickers quickly. This cellophane gift bag shimmers with holographic stars cut from adhesive-backed holographic paper, using a home die-cut system.

Photocopied Heart-in-Hand Sticker

Consider creating a truly unique sticker by photocopying line art onto adhesive-backed transparency paper. Cut out the images, then apply them onto interesting paper that shows through in between the line art. Here, a traditional "heart-in-hand" image is given graphic punch by laying it over contrasting checkered papers.

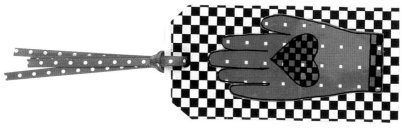

3-D Party Sticker

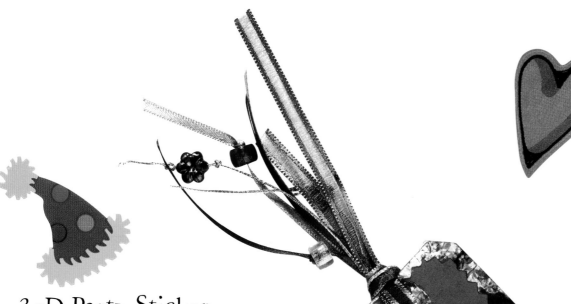

Double-sided tape can be transformed into a sticker. It is available in sheet form, on rolls in varying widths, and in die-cut shapes. As shown on this tag, it is used as a border and covered with crafter's foil.

Three-dimensional, double-adhesive-backed foam lettering creates a dimensional sticker. Remove the release paper and apply onto the desired surface. Remove the top layer of release paper and cover the sticky letter with crafter's foil as shown at right. Tiny holeless beads, glitter, or flocking are also good options.

Establishing a Look or Mood

The vast array of stickers available today is astounding. The stickers you choose for your projects will help determine their style. In fact, there is no faster way to establish a look or mood for a project than with stickers. In this chapter, you will see a variety of projects that showcase a wide range of styles to help you get a sense of the range of looks you can achieve: a simple elegant Christmas card, stunning wedding stationery, rustic warmth in a winter scrapbook page, a delicate shabby-chic serving tray, a vintage ladylike shadow box.

project . . .
Joy Card

Whether you are designing a room or creating a greeting card, one of your primary goals is to establish a mood. Color, pattern, and accents are the tools you use to set the tone. Here soft sage greens, cranberry, and gold establish a lovely Christmas feel. The intricately cut gold letter stickers provide the classic elegance to really set this card apart.

Instructions:

1. Cut darker sage cardstock to size of card front. Adhere onto front of card.

2. Cut cranberry cardstock to desired size. Adhere onto sage cardstock.

3. Using craft knife and cutting board, cut light sage cardstock slightly smaller than cranberry piece. Cut three equally sized and spaced windows into light sage piece, slightly larger than lettering. Adhere onto cranberry cardstock.

4. Apply gold letters into windows. Apply gold borders as desired.

Materials

Card

Cardstocks: cranberry; two shades of sage green

Paper adhesive

Stickers: gold borders; gold lettering

Tools

Craft knife

Cutting board

Paper cutter

———— design tip ————➤

Beautiful alphabet stickers can turn a plain card into elegant, personalized stationery. Create a coordinating pack of cards and tie them with a pretty ribbon for a thoughtful gift.

project . . .
Wedding Stationery

Instructions:

1. Using computer, type text and print onto scrap paper to preview. Change font and layout until satisfied.

Note: Font used in photograph is Edwardian Script.

2. Cut cream cardstock and vellum to 6¼" × 8".

3. Print finalized text onto cream cardstock.

4. Apply vellum adhesive onto top and bottom edges of vellum and adhere onto cream cardstock, covering text, for invitation.

5. Apply stickers onto invitation.

6. Cut ivory cardstock to 6¾" × 8½".

7. Center and adhere invitation onto ivory cardstock with paper adhesive.

8. Cut second cream cardstock to 7¼" × 9".

9. Center and adhere invitation with ivory border onto cream cardstock.

Materials

Botanical stickers
Cardstocks: cream (2); ivory
Gold-printed vellum
Paper adhesive
Scrap paper
Vellum adhesive

Tools

Computer with word-processing program and printer
Paper cutter
Ruler

⟶ design tip ⟶

Creating satin-ribbon corners for your invitation or stationery is simple. Cut a 2" piece of ribbon. Tape a small piece of double-sided tape to the inside ends. Wrap the ribbon around the corner of the card and secure the ends to the back of the card so that they lay flat. The length of ribbon needed is twice the width of the ribbon (e.g. cut 1"-wide ribbon to 2" in length).

What could be more elegant than coordinated formal wedding invitations, place cards, album, and thank-you notes? This exquisite set was made with lovely papers and stickers.

Creating a complete wedding stationery ensemble is easy, inexpensive, and best of all, you will love your customized creations.

There are a couple of tricks to achieving elegance with stickers:

- Choose beautiful images and pair them with coordinating papers.
- Layer papers for a rich look.
- Add touches of elegance, such as the satin corners on the album.
- Remember that "less is more" when going for an elegant look.
- Wedding stationery generally requires a limited color palette; two to three colors at the most.
- Tone-on-tone color palettes are particularly effective.

project . . .
Decoupage Tray

Love the look of collage and looking for a way to incorporate it into a pretty piece for your home? Stickers are the answer! Stickers can work beautifully on surfaces you may never have considered, such as wood, ceramics, glass, and plastic. To make them more durable, seal them with a sealer appropriate to the surface you have selected.

This shabby-chic tray would be a lovely addition to a bedroom or sunroom.

Instructions:

1. Paint tray with ivory. Let dry completely.

2. Using sandpaper, distress tray.

3. Apply wash of diluted burnt-umber pigment. Let dry completely.

4. Using sandpaper, gently distress papers and stickers.

5. Cut papers into desired shapes.

6. Adhere papers onto tray with decoupage medium. Let dry for 20 minutes.

7. Apply stickers onto tray as desired.

8. Seal entire tray with decoupage medium. Let dry for 20 minutes and repeat. Let project cure for four weeks before using.

Materials

Assorted decorative papers
Assorted stickers
Burnt-umber pigment
Ivory paint
Matte-finish decoupage medium
Wooden tray

Tools

Decorative-edged scissors
Foam brushes (2)
Sandpaper

————design tip————▶ For additional protection against moisture and water spots, apply a coating of furniture wax.

Winter Memories Page

The star of this page is the large photo placed in the center. Soft pine branch patterns appear in the vellum and underlying woven paper that are layered under the picture.

Stickers add the necessary bold dashes of pattern to the pages. Pine branches and berries adorn the sticker photo corners, journaling border, and page border, adding strong pattern in small doses.

Shadow Box

To establish a vintage ladies' assemblage look, I used photographs tucked into a ribbon lattice as focal points in this shadow box. Beautiful papers, based on vintage fabrics, are a perfect place to begin to build the scene. An old letter, antique perfume labels, a tiny brass frame, and old earrings (actually buttons with the shanks removed) add interest.

Vellum lace border stickers encircle the mat opening, drawing attention to the box. Rose stickers, based on old botanical paintings, are purposely placed partially off the mat and overhanging the box. This adds interest to the frame and draws the eye into the main attraction, the shadow box.

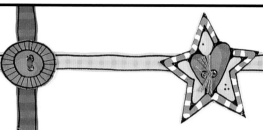

Combining Images

It has been said that the whole is greater than the sum of its parts. This is certainly true when you are crafting with stickers. Combining various sticker images can help you create a truly unique and memorable project. In this chapter, you will see how to:

create a new image by combining many smaller images, isolate and use part of an image, and add invidivual images together to create scenes.

Please join us for an
OPEN HOUSE
Sunday, May 3rd
1:00-5:00 p.m.
64 Oak Street

So plans were drawn,
and paint was selected
and money was spent,
and spent, and spent!

project . . .
Wedding Scrapbook Page

Instructions:

1. Cut pink and light silver papers in graduated sizes to create frames for title and basket.

2. Adhere frames and photographs onto page.

3. Create basket by placing stencil on light-box. Place paper over stencils and burnish design with stylus. Cut out basket.

4. Center and adhere basket onto frame.

5. Apply lettering onto frame.

6. Apply ribbons and roses as desired.

Notes: To create the balance, height, width, and dimension of the basket pictured here, tuck individual roses into (behind) the basket. Vary the height so that they look more natural, beginning with the tallest first.

Next, add the roses that are spilling out of the sides of the basket. Create depth and dimension by bumping out several individual blossoms in the foreground with small pieces of foam tape.

Curl other blooms and leaves forward with your finger and powder these protruding images so that they are more likely to keep their new shape and do not stick to the page.

Finish by placing individual blossoms into empty spaces.

—————design tips —————→

Materials

12"-square silver paper
Brass basket stencil
Foam tape
Large photograph
Papers: pink; light silver
Paper adhesive
Stickers: basket; border; lettering; ribbons; roses

Tools

Craft scissors
Embossing stylus
Light-box

All papers used on the page complement the soft gray tones of the photograph. Only the roses stand out as an accent color.

Tying an element from the page—in this case, the roses—into the title helps integrate it into the entire page and provides an unexpected visual surprise.

To keep the eye flowing around the page, let the roses trail over the edges of the title and basket.

Feel free to cut, fold, or reshape a sticker so that it works for your particular needs. In this case, the ribbon that the rose basket is hanging from was actually designed to be one long relatively straight ribbon. By folding it in half, a hanging picture ribbon was created.

Sometimes less is more—sometimes it's not. There are occasions when one balloon will not suffice—you need an armful. A molehill is not the look you are going for in this project—you need a mountain. So, how do you create a mountain out of a molehill, a gigantic balloon bouquet from a lone balloon, a basketful of roses when you only have individual blossoms? Combining small individual images to create a new larger image is simple.

project . . .
"You're a Doll" Tag

Tag art is a really trendy look today. This charming gift card takes tag art one step further by creating a pocket on the tag. A bouquet of sticker flowers is tucked into this pocket; but lollipops, photographs, or a gift certificate would be welcome surprises, too.

Instructions:

1. Draw desired tag and pocket on checkered paper; then cut out.

2. Adhere pieces onto cardstock, leaving enough room to draw pocket flap. Draw flap and cut out all pieces.

3. Adhere pocket onto tag, leaving the top unattached.

4. Set eyelets onto top of tag and pocket flap.

5. Draw stitch lines around tag, pocket, and flap as desired.

6. Adhere flap onto front of pocket.

7. Apply stickers onto cardstock and cut out.

8. Attach cutouts onto tag with foam tape.

Note: Tuck flowers into pocket to look as though they are growing.

9. Thread ribbon through eyelet.

Materials

Blue checkered paper
Decorative eyelets (2)
Foam tape
Paper adhesive
Ribbon
Stickers: doll; flowers; star; title
White cardstock

Tools

Black felt-tipped marker
Craft scissors
Eyelet setter
Hammer
Hole punch
Pencil

——design tip——→

While this tag is designed to be child-like and adorable, varying the paper choice and pocket shape could alter the tone of it completely. Try using a piece of paper lace on a narrower pocket that comes to a point for a Victorian look, or a piece of woven fabric accented by a piece of rawhide and a turquoise bead for a Southwestern look.

project . . .
Window Box

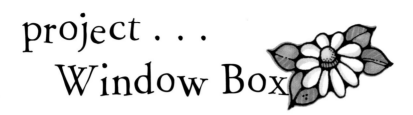

Instructions:

1. Cut two 3½" × 5" pieces from cardstock.

2. Draw a four-square window pattern onto top ⅔ of one piece. Using craft knife, cut out "panes" Use this piece as a pattern and repeat on second piece of cardstock.

3. Adhere panes together, with transparency paper sandwiched in between.

4. To create window box, cut 3½" × 1½" block from floral foam.

5. Cut strips of cardstock to wrap around sides and bottom of foam and attach with double-sided tape. Cut front and back panel from cardstock and adhere onto front and back of foam.

6. Attach window box onto bottom of window with double-sided tape.

7. Adhere crepe paper onto floral foam.

8. Apply insect and flower stickers onto cardstock and cut out.

9. Attach flowers onto toothpicks with foam tape. Push toothpicks into foam.

10. Attach insects onto window as desired.

Materials

Double-sided tape
Floral foam
Foam tape
Green toothpicks
Paper adhesive
Shredded yellow crepe paper
Stickers: flowers; frame; insects
Transparency paper: 3½" × 5"
White cardstock

Tools

Craft knife
Craft scissors

——— design tips ———→

Creative ways to use this window box include writing names onto the front and using as a place card or adding a magnet onto the back.

Make the project larger sized and add photographs in the windows, then display as a springtime photograph frame.

This decorative window box is a great way to use
stickers to add dimension to a project in a new way.

project . . .
House-shaped Invitation

In the world of stickers, you can have your cake and eat it, too! Just because the sticker was created to be used one way, doesn't mean that you can't use it in an entirely different context.

Instructions:

1. Using paper cutter, cut cardstocks into two equally sized black rectangles for house, four yellow triangles for roof, two red rectangles for chimney, two red squares for windows, and one red rectangle for door.

2. Using punch, punch along left-hand edge of house pieces.

3. For front cover, adhere one roof piece onto top of black rectangle, overlapping the pieces a bit. Turn house over. Adhere chimney onto back side of roof.

4. Adhere second roof piece directly over first, hiding chimney and house edges. Repeat for back cover.

5. Trim left corner from roof overhang on back cover to match left edge of house so it doesn't interfere with page turning.

6. Adhere door and windows onto house front.

7. Apply stickers: buttons serve as doorknobs, borders become windowpanes, perennial garden borders are trimmed to become window boxes, and tree stickers are cut into topiaries.

Materials

Bookbinding disks
Cardstocks: black; red; yellow
Paper adhesive
Photographs and memorabilia
Stickers: buttons; construction; hearts; moving day; thin borders; perennial garden borders; small trees; wildflowers

Tools

Bookbinding punch
Computer with word-processing program and printer
Craft scissors
Paper cutter

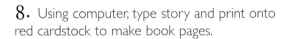

8. Using computer, type story and print onto red cardstock to make book pages.

9. Trim pages slightly smaller than house to fit inside for book pages.

10. Punch along left hand edge of pages.

11. Lay out pages in appropriate order.

12. Adhere photographs and memorabilia onto pages without text.

13. Apply stickers onto inside of book as desired.

14. Insert bookbinding disks through all pages and covers of book.

So plans were drawn, and paint was selected and money was spent, and spent, and spent!

Please join us for an OPEN HOUSE Sunday, May 3rd 1:00-5:00 p.m. 64 Oak Street

Dimension

While some stickers available today are dimensional novelties, most stickers are still flat. This chapter will show you many ways to add dimension and texture including: folding stickers to create pop-ups and free-standing elements; adding thickness to a sticker so that it can be bent or molded; layering stickers to create a multilevel scene; popping out stickers from a page.

project . . .
Birdhouse Journal

This charming accordion journal incorporates varying levels of dimension. You can make your own journal or buy one that is premade at your favorite craft store.

Instructions:

1. Cut two 6" squares from paper and adhere one square onto each cover, folding and adhering excess toward inside.

2. Using craft scissors, cut front cover borders to desired size and shape from yellow and blue cardstocks and adhere borders onto cover.

3. Apply stickers onto second blue cardstock and cut out stickers, leaving small border around images.

4. Stack 2–4 pieces of foam tape together and apply onto backs of stickers.

5. Attach stickers onto front cover.

Materials

5"-square accordion journal
Blue plaid paper (2)
Cardstocks: blue (2); white (8); yellow
Foam tape
Paper adhesive
Ribbon
Stickers: birdhouses; birds; flowers; hearts

Tools

Craft scissors
Paper cutter
Ruler

In the project pictured here, the center birdhouse is "popped out" farthest from background with three layers of foam tape behind it, as opposed to two layers behind the other birdhouses.

Sides of pink and green birdhouses are bent slightly and secured onto journal cover with tiny pieces of foam tape. This produces a rounded effect to birdhouses.

The bird's body is attached with three layers of foam tape, while bird's wings are attached with four layers, seemingly extended in flight.

——— design tip ———→

project . . .
Winter Scene Gift Box

Stickers are the perfect element for creating a dimensional scene. The winter scene on this gift box is captivating from every angle.

Instructions:

1. Apply stickers of penguins and snowmen onto their mirror images, back to back, pressing images together except for bottoms.

2. Apply penguin feet onto box top. Attach snowmen bottoms onto box top with foam tape.

3. Fold two tree stickers in half and remove release paper. Adhere right-hand back of one onto left-hand back of other. Repeat with two more tree stickers.

4. Adhere doubled trees back to back, creating one tree. Attach trees onto box top with foam tape.

5. Cut 1" piece from foam tape for wagon

6. Cut two pieces from white paper to fit top and bottom of wagon.

7. Apply green borders onto wagon sides.

Materials

Foam tape
Gift box
Stickers: green border; penguins; picket fence; snowflakes; snowmen; trees; wheels
White paper

Tool

Craft scissors

8. Cut eight small pieces of foam tape and stack together in two separate stacks of four. Attach onto bottom of wagon in front and back wheel position. Attach wagon onto box.

9. Apply wheels onto wagon to cover stacked tape.

10. Apply snowflakes and picket fence onto box as desired.

———design tip———➤ Techniques used on this box can be used on a holiday mantel, table centerpiece, or inside a shadow box.

project . . .
Garden Journal

Instructions:

1. Cut paper 1" smaller all around than journal cover and adhere onto journal cover.

2. Apply denim and bandana borders onto edges of paper cover.

3. Apply denim pocket onto white cardstock. Trim away extra cardstock from pocket edges.

4. Apply letter and grommet stickers onto pocket.

5. Using hand, curve pocket slightly.

6. Apply thick craft glue onto sides and bottom edges of pocket and adhere onto cover so pocket is slightly bent, leaving a space between pocket and journal. Hold pocket until glue sets.

7. Fold seed packet in half and cut away most of packet just beyond fold. This will minimize bulk of seed packet so it fits into pocket more easily.

8. Adhere bandana sticker onto paper so it looks like it is tucked into pocket.

9. Apply thick craft glue onto back of seed packet and bottom of spade. Insert into pocket. Let glue dry completely.

Materials

Kraft-paper-covered journal
Paper adhesive
Red grid-lined paper
Seed packet
Small spade
Stickers: bandana; bandana border; denim border; denim pocket; letters; grommet
Thick craft glue
White cardstock

Tools

Craft scissors
Ruler

———design tip———→

Using the same pocket sticker, change the theme of the journal by replacing the garden tools with small cooking utensils and a tiny jar of hot sauce for a cook's journal; tea bags, a small pen, and a pair of doll's eyeglasses for a personal thoughts journal; toy airplane, miniature passport, and a dollar bill from a foreign country for a travel journal.

Check out dollhouse supply stores for charming theme-related miniatures that make great pocket stuffers.

By applying the sticker onto cardstock and trimming the cardstock to the dimensions of the sticker, you can create a very sturdy paper embellishment. Use this technique when creating small journal covers, free-hanging embellishments for cards, and moveable elements in kinetic books, cards, and pockets as seen on this journal.

project . . .
Adventure Scrapbook Page

Instructions:

1. Cut out tree and adhere onto page.

2. Using decorative scissors, cut paper to desired size to border photograph. Adhere border onto page and adhere photograph onto border.

3. Cut cardstock to desired size to border title. Adhere lettering onto cardstock.

4. Using $\frac{1}{8}$" hole punch, punch holes in four corners of cardstock and set eyelets.

5. Thread small piece of twine through eyelets and leave ends loose.

6. Adhere cardstock onto page.

7. Using $\frac{1}{16}$" hole punch, punch holes into page, just under eyelets.

8. Thread loose ends of twine through $\frac{1}{16}$" holes and tape ends onto back of page.

9. Punch leaf shapes from all three colors of construction paper. Fold leaves in half and glue onto page as desired.

10. Apply ladybug stickers onto page. Apply frog, squirrel, and fly stickers onto a piece of foam tape. Attach stickers onto page.

11. Cut bear's legs apart and feed through tire, apply foam tape onto bear and tire.

12. Glue small piece of rope from tree in arc.

13. Attach bear and tire onto page.

14. Fold legs of cropped photograph and tape photograph onto platform.

Materials

$\frac{1}{8}$" green eyelets (4)
12"-square dark green paper
Cellophane tape
Construction papers: green; light green; yellow
Corrugated cardstock
Decorative paper
Foam tape
Glue
Paper adhesive
Photographs cropped from background: group; one person standing
Stickers: bear; flies; frogs; ladybugs; lettering; squirrel; tire; tree with platform
Thin rope
Twine

Tools

Craft scissors
Decorative scissors
Eyelet setter
Hammer
Hole punches: $\frac{1}{16}$"; $\frac{1}{8}$"; leaf-shaped

When you add texture to stickers, you add an entirely new layer of surprise and interest to your page. There are so many creative ways to give your stickers a little three-dimensional appeal.

project . . .
3-D Easter Scene

Instructions:

Note: This project is assembled in five layers and glued together once all the layers are completely decorated.

Layer #1 (back)

1. Glue blue cardstock onto back of one foam-core frame.

2. Apply grass onto front of cardstock ¼" above frame edge.

3. Apply eggs and butterfly onto front of cardstock.

Layer #2

1. Tape transparency paper onto back of second foam-core frame.

2. Apply fence, chick, and egg onto front of transparency paper along frame edge.

Layer #3

1. Tape transparency paper onto back of third foam-core frame.

2. Cut ¼" from bottoms of grass. Apply grass, bunny with basket, eggs, and butterflies onto front of transparency paper.

Layer #4

1. Tape transparency paper onto back of fourth foam-core frame.

2. Cut ½" from bottoms of grass. Apply grass tops, eggs, and butterfly onto transparency paper.

Materials

½"-wide masking tape

Cardstocks: light blue, 7½" × 6"; purple, 7½" × 6"

Easter stickers: butterflies; chicks, eggs; fence; flower; grass; large bunny with basket; leaf; thin purple border

Foam-core board frames, 7½" × 6" (5)

Foam tape

Green embossed-paper frame with 5" × 3" oval center

Transparency paper, 7" × 5" (4)

White craft glue

Tools

Craft knife
Cutting board

Layer #5 (front)

1. Glue purple cardstock onto remaining foam-core frame. Place cardstock side down on cutting board.

2. Using craft knife, cut center from cardstock along inside edges of frame.

3. Center embossed frame onto purple frame.

4. Embellish with flower, leaf, grass, and purple border stickers as shown in photo on page 45.

5. Attach one flower onto floral embellishment with foam tape.

6. Glue all layers together.

Do you remember peering into candy Easter egg scenes as a child? The miniature world created in those eggs was fascinating. Here is a technique that creates the same effect using stickers and paper.

project . . .
Springtime Gift Tag

To create a unique embellishment that pops right off the page, try this "back-to-back" sticker trick.

Begin by selecting a fairly symmetrical sticker; hearts, simple trees, presents, and flowers, all work well. As you can see from the tag pictured here, the flowers popping out of the envelope aren't completely symmetrical yet it works with this technique.

Instructions:

1. Remove release paper from stickers. Gently bend stickers and adhere left-hand back half of one sticker onto right-hand back half of second sticker. Half of each sticker should remain exposed.

2. Adhere exposed side of third sticker onto exposed half of first. Trim off any small portion of the sticker backs that show through to the front.

3. Pull apart exposed side of stickers and apply onto tag.

4. Stamp message and tie ribbons onto tag.

Materials

Decorative ribbons
Symmetrical stickers (3)
Tag

Tools

Craft scissors
Ink pad
Rubber stamp with message

————design tips————▶

The pop-out technique used on this tag is a great way to give an element on a card a lot of focus. Simply create a flat background on the card with stickers, then apply the pop-out over the background. Try having an animal pop out from a jungle background, Santa stand by a Christmas tree, or pop out a phrase such as Happy Birthday from a background of confetti, streamers, and balloons. If a little bit of the supporting side pieces of sticker show in a way that detracts from the center sticker, simply snip a bit of them away.

Changing the Look of a Sticker

With a little time and creativity, we can change the look of a sticker to customize it for our needs, allowing us to get the exact look we want and create something very original. Some of the techniques covered in this chapter include: altering the surface of a sticker with embossing powders, pearlescent and glitter paints, and tiny holeless beads; using the underside of a sticker; customizing the color of a sticker with chalks, pencils, and inks; applying a high-gloss sheen; aging a sticker with color and crackle effects.

project . . .
Floral Photo Mat

Instructions:

1. Cut tan cardstock slightly smaller than dimensions of frame top.

2. Cut mulberry paper 1" larger than frame top on all sides.

3. Adhere mulberry paper onto frame top.

4. Using craft knife, cut "x" in mulberry paper at center of frame.

5. Fold and adhere all paper edges onto back of frame top.

6. Using sunflower ink, color-tint mulberry paper edges.

7. Apply floral stickers onto tan cardstock frame. Try to cover entire surface.

8. Using cotton swabs with parchment and rose-colored inks, color in flowers and leaves. Use tissue paper to apply inks adding texture to frame. Continue adding colors until you are pleased with design.

Note: Precise color placement can be achieved by using a cotton swab to apply the ink colors. In broader parts of the flowers, try using a crumpled tissue to apply ink colors to achieve a more textured appearance.

Materials

Beige mulberry paper
Clear embossing powder
Floral stickers
Paper adhesive
Pigment inks: parchment, sunflower, rose
Square picture frame
Tan cardstock
White crafter's glue

Tools

Cotton swabs
Craft scissors
Craft knife
Heat gun
Tissue paper

9. Heat-emboss floral frame with clear embossing powder.

10. Repeat previous step, building up layers of clear embossing powder.

11. Adhere floral frame onto frame top.

→ design tip →

When coloring flowers, remember that the petals are colored more intensely in the center of the flowers. The color, generally, becomes less concentrated as you move out from the center into the tips of the petals.

Sometimes a sticker isn't quite the right color to match a particular photograph or background paper you have chosen. Changing the colors on a sticker is easy and produces beautiful results. Two photo mats have been created—one with the stickers as they are manufactured as shown below on the frame, and the other with stickers that have been touched up with pigment-inks. Try watercolor paints, colored pencils, or chalks to embellish or alter the look of a sticker. When using chalks to color stickers, seal them with a spray sealer after coloring to preserve them.

project . . .
Ballet Recital

Okay, let's test your powers of observation. Where are the stickers on this page? And, I'm not talking about the little flower and ribbon stickers you see. Give up? The stickers are used on the underside of the page, underneath the holes that have been punched. The sticky side of the sticker peaks through the holes and catches glitter sprinkled on top.

Instructions:

1. Print title onto one edge of white cardstock.

2. Trim title card to desired size. Cut one edge of blue cardstock to ½" larger all around than title card. Adhere title card onto blue card.

3. Using ¹⁄₁₆" hole punch, punch an even number of holes around edge of title card.

4. Starting in center top, begin lacing ribbon around card edge. Thread ribbon ends through top two holes twice so ends come out in front of card. Tie small bow.

5. Adhere title card onto checkered paper for page.

6. Adhere photographs onto remaining white cardstock and crop around images.

7. Cut three equally sized pieces from white cardstock. Cut three pieces from remaining blue cardstock to ½" larger than white pieces.

8. Using ¼" and ⅛" hole punches, randomly punch two white pieces.

9. Apply sticker scraps onto backs of punched pieces so sticky side shows through holes.

10. Apply glitter into sticky holes. Tap off excess glitter and save for another use.

11. Trim edges of one blue piece with scallop-edged scissors.

12. Using ¹⁄₁₆" hole punch, punch center of each scallop.

13. Adhere unpunched white piece onto scallop-edged blue piece. Adhere punched pieces onto remaining blue pieces.

14. Adhere one image onto each white piece.

15. Position and adhere matted images onto page.

16. Apply flowers and hearts onto page as desired.

Materials

⅛"-wide pink satin ribbon
12"-square pink checkered scrapbook paper
Cardstocks: delft blue (2); white (2)
Paper adhesive
Photographs that can be cropped (3)
Pink ultrafine glitter
Stickers: flowers;
hearts; paper scraps

Tools

Craft scissors
Hole punches: ¹⁄₁₆"; ⅛"; ¼"
Paper cutter
Pen
Scallop-edged scissors

Susannah's Ballet Recital
June 2003

———design tip———➤ When creating a small card laced with ribbon, make certain to punch an even number of holes that line up neatly opposite one another. That way, the ribbon stitches look balanced and both ribbon ends wind up in the front of the card, ready to tie into a bow.

project . . .
Treasure Chest

Instructions:

1. Paint entire box with gesso. Let dry completely.

Note: If box has hardware, cover before painting.

2. Paint box with cream. Let dry completely.

3. Using photograph as guide, apply stickers onto box. Use self-adhesive notes to mask off edge of box.

4. Paint edge of box with brown acrylic paint. Let dry completely.

5. Stamp text with crafter's ink inside masked frame and dry with heat gun.

6. Apply Step 1 of the crackle finish kit onto entire box, following manufacturer's directions. Wait recommended time to allow it to dry.

7. Apply Step 2 of crackle finish kit and allow it to dry completely.

8. Dilute dark brown acrylic paint—⅓ water to ⅔ paint. Using small rag, apply diluted paint mixture onto small portion of box. Wipe off excess paint with separate slightly damp rag.

Materials

Acrylic matte varnish

Acrylic paints: brown; dark brown; cream

Crafter's ink

Decorative stickers

Fine-crackle finish kit

White acrylic gesso

Wooden box

Tools

Foam brush

Flower rubber stamp

Heat Gun

Paintbrushes (3)

Self-adhesive notes

Small rags (2)

Note: Make certain to remove only the excess paint. The desired effect is to have brown paint gather in the cracks of the finish. Continue with this process until box is completed.

9. Apply coat of varnish onto entire box with foam brush. Let dry completely. Remove any covering from hardware.

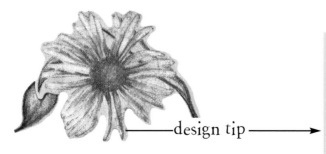

— design tip —➤

Rubber stamps that look like an allover crackle finish are popular today. Stamping onto a sticker with a faux-crackle rubber stamp and brown ink will produce a similar, albeit one-dimensional, effect to a real crackle finish kit.

Sometimes a project will call for a more antique, weathered look. You can apply aging techniques to stickers, as well as to the surfaces they are on.

Applying a crackle finish and a light wash of brown acrylic paint will add instant decades to a piece, giving it a warm, antique appearance.

project . . .
Small Gift Cards

Here is a great way to create a quick and easy gift card that has a lot of style. Apply a sticker to a small folded card. Embellish the sticker with any one of a myriad of surface embellishment products available today. They add texture as well as glitter and sparkle. Make certain you let them dry completely before handling.

Daisy Card

This daisy really shines with yellow glitter glue applied onto the flower center in small dots and spread with long strokes onto the petals.

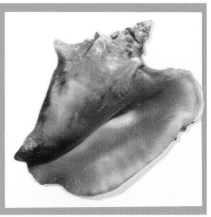

Seashell Card

This seashell's surface is given a slightly rough texture, as well as a bit of shine by adding frosted crystal embossing powder.

Rose Card

Glitter glue, spread thin with a paintbrush makes this single rose look dewy fresh.

Pansy Card

The details of the pansy are accented with purple iridescent glue and clear dimensional acrylic glaze, adding sparkle and texture.

Birthday Card

This cake says "party!" Several colors of glitter glue and white pearlescent paint add jazzy decorations that rival the best of bakeries.

Glinda Card

Glinda, the Good Witch really arrives in style with the addition of glitter and tiny crystals glued on with a dot of craft glue.

Daffodil Bouquet Card

A daffodil bouquet goes from pretty to spectacular with the addition of tiny colorless beads. Apply clear extra-strong beading tape over the portion of the sticker you want to bead. Trim off any excess. Pour on the beads, saving any extras that don't stick to the tape for another project.

Wedding Card

This wedding cake looks good enough to eat. It receives its added texture and sparkle from pearlescent and glitter glue.

Borders and Frames

Sticker borders and frames are handy for encircling a photo or finishing a page, but their versatility goes way beyond these obvious uses. In fact, you may find yourself reaching for your border and frame stickers more often than any other type of sticker in your collection once you check out the unique ideas covered in this chapter, which include: weaving stickers together for an eye-catching background, creating border "fabric" and punching out elements from this "fabric", border quilting, crafting borders from individual sticker images, kaleidescope frames, tiny framed shadow boxes.

project . . .
Daisy Card

While there are numerous border sticker choices available today, sometimes you just can't find the perfect one for a particular project. Look to your individual image stickers for the solution.

Instructions:

1. Draw straight line through center of daisies. Cut daisies in half.

2. Apply daisies onto card around center opening varying the colors and overlapping slightly.

3. Cut borders to size of window opening. Apply borders around edges, covering cut edge of daisies.

4. Apply message onto front of card

5. Tape photograph onto inside of card with image showing through opening.

6. Refold card.

Materials

Cellophane tape
Photograph
Square trifold photograph card
Stickers: gerbera daisies; message; thin border

Tools

Craft scissors
Pencil
Ruler

—— design tip ——→ Apply coordinating stickers onto an envelope to match the card.

project . . .
Framed Sticker Quilt

Quilting is one of our country's most beloved craft forms. The endless possibilities of repeated patterns and colors are sheer delight. You can create those same patterns with stickers. Simply lay border stickers down on paper, side by side, to create your "fabric." Then cut out geometric shapes from this sticker "fabric" and play with their placement until you achieve a pleasing design.

Instructions:

1. Cut tan-on-tan paper into approximately 6" square.

2. Apply border stickers onto one long edge of cardstock next to each other until they are at least 2" in width, making certain no cardstock shows in between.

3. Cut eight equally sized triangles from cardstock/stickers.

4. Lay out and adhere triangles onto tan-on-tan square for quilt center.

Note: Lay out similar designs opposite each other.

5. Cut remaining papers into progressively larger squares. Layer and adhere under quilt center.

6. Frame as desired.

Materials

Cardstock

Differently patterned border stickers in similar tones (4–5)

Paper adhesive

Papers: plum; shimmery rose; tan; tan-on-tan

Picture frame

Tools

Paper cutter

Ruler

—— design tip ——→

Once border stickers have been applied onto cardstock, they can be cut into any desired shape using scissors or decorative punches. Look at quilt books for pattern ideas.

project . . .
Bobbi and Jim Scrapbook Page

Instructions:

1. Cut gauzy paper to 11½" square.

2. Center and adhere gauzy paper onto scrapbook paper and adhere.

3. Cut decorative paper and second gauzy paper in graduated sizes large enough to border photograph.

4. Adhere photograph onto page.

5. Begin applying border stickers around photograph by measuring border stickers so they are dimensions of photo edge plus width of border sticker, doubled. For instance, if the photograph is 4" wide and border sticker is ½" wide, border length would need to be 4"+½"+½" = 5". Place one patterned border around each side of photograph, overlapping border edges.

Note: The edges should be double thickness because of overlap.

6. Place tip of craft knife on inside corner of border sticker where it meets corner of photograph. Gently draw tip across top layer of border to outside corner of border. Remove small piece you have just cut out, mitering corner. Proceed to miter other three corners.

7. Add next border just outside first border.

Note: Remember, new width is that of photograph plus width of border already in place, doubled.

Materials

12"-square decorative gauzy paper (2)
12"-square pale rose scrapbook paper
Brass corner embellishments (4)
Craft glue
Decorative paper
Large photograph
Paper adhesive
Patterned border stickers in coordinating colors (4)

Tools

Computer with word-processing program and printer
Craft knife
Paper cutter
Ruler
Toothpicks

8. Repeat Step 6 to miter all four corners.

9. Create title on computer and print onto decorative paper, then cut out title.

10. Cut decorative paper and gauzy paper in graduated sizes so they serve as mats for title.

11. Using paper adhesive, adhere each layer of paper down, centering title on top.

12. Using toothpick, apply craft glue onto brass corner embellishments and apply onto corners of photo borders.

Mitering is a technique that makes border stickers look perfectly joined at the corners rather than overlapped. It lends a professional polish to a bordered element on a page. When using border stickers that are patterned, mitering allows for an unbroken line in the pattern to continue all around the framed element, adding a lot of visual punch.

project . . .
Autumn Scrapbook Page

Instructions for page:

1. Adhere vellum and borders onto cream cardstock.

2. Adhere netting onto page.

3. Center and adhere photographs onto frame stickers.

4. Write journaling onto blank frame sticker.

5. Adhere photograph and journaling frames onto page.

6. Tie twine onto page.

Materials

Cardstocks: 12"-square cream; green
Craft glue
Foam tape
Natural netting
Paper adhesive
Photographs
Small trinket
Stickers: borders that coordinate with vellum; coordinating autumn frames in different sizes; leaves
Twine: tan; white
Vellum adhesive
Vellums: coordinating pattern; light brown

Tools

Craft knife
Cutting board
Marker
Paper cutter

Instructions for shadow box:

1. Apply frame onto green cardstock. Cut away excess cardstock, leaving narrow edge all around.

2. Using craft knife, cut out center of frame.

3. Apply frame center onto additional piece of cardstock that is slightly smaller than frame

4. Glue charm onto frame center.

5. Apply thin strips double-layered of foam tape onto back of frame.

6. Attach frame over frame center.

7. Trim off any excess tape that may be showing beyond edges.

8. Glue shadow box onto page.

The first sticker frames in existence were the all-too-familiar "Hello, My name is . . ." name tags. We've all had to wear them at one point or another. Today, sticker frames are a convenient, timesaving device for scrapbooking. There are several clever ways to put these frames to use.

project . . .
Bath Salts Jar

Instructions:

1. Wash and dry jar and lid thoroughly

2. Fill jar with handmade product as desired.

Note: Make your own bath salts with instructions below.

3. Write on frame as desired.

4. Apply frame onto jar.

5. Cut fabric into circle approximately 1" larger all around than jar lid.

6. Secure fabric in place over lid with rubber band.

7. Tie ribbons around lid to cover rubber band.

Materials

Coarse Epsom or sea salts
Fabric
Frame sticker
Jar with lid
Liquid food coloring
Perfumed oils
Ribbons
Rubber band

Tools

Craft scissors
Decorative-edged scissors
Pen

Instructions for bath salts:

1. Mix course Epsom or sea salts in bowl with several drops of food coloring.

2. Stir together thoroughly.

3. Add several drops of perfumed oil until scent is pleasantly strong.

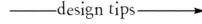
————design tips————→

Adding fragrance to your bath salts is a lovely addition. Perfumed oils can be found in the soap-making section of your local craft store. Add several drops to begin with until you have a pleasantly strong fragrance. Use a funnel to scoop the bath salts into a narrow-necked bottle.

Use sticker frames as labels on handmade jarred
food such as jam, applesauce, or chocolate sauce,
or on handmade bath products such as lotions
or the bath salts described on page 68.

Frames on place cards and tags

Frame stickers can be used on a variety of projects. Using coordinating stickers on various items ties the items together nicely.

Apply a sticker onto a folded piece of coordinating cardstock to create place cards for a dinner party.

Turn sticker frames into gift tags by applying them onto coordinating cardstock cut into the shape of a tag. Punch a hole and thread with a piece of ribbon.

Susanna Turns 1 Scrapbook Page

In this scrapbook page, borders are used traditionally to frame the large white card. They are also used in several unique ways:

• The photograph is framed against a backdrop weaving created by borders. Weave the borders together onto a piece of waxed paper until desired size. Borders can be tightly woven so that no background space is visible or loosely woven, as they are here. Once you are satisfied, lift the border weaving off the waxed paper and place it onto the page.

• The decorative hearts embellishing the journaling are also created with borders. Lay borders side by side on a sheet of scrap paper. Punch, die-cut, or hand-cut the shapes of your choice.

• Create confetti by cutting tiny squares from border stickers and applying them onto the page.

Kaleidoscope Frames

Create a kaleidoscope effect with frame stickers by mounting coordinating sticker frames of different sizes and shapes on top of each other. Fit matching photo corners into the right angles created by the layered frames. Frame as desired. Here, two sticker frames and eight corner stickers are used with two contrasting papers.

Sweet 15 Scrapbook Page

Vellum stickers printed on clear plastic sheets are becoming very popular. On this page, journaling is framed with the rectangular vellum stickers. Large pink rhinestones add dimension and a touch of glamour to the page. Coordinating scrapbook papers work well with the matching stickers to tie the whole look together.

Using Stickers More Creatively

I like to think of these creative techniques as ways to think outside of the box. Use the ideas here as a springboard for your own experimentation. In this chapter, I will show you techniques including: using stickers as die-cuts, new uses for office supply stickers, changing the look of a single sticker—12 different ways, letting your stickers help you play dress-up, discovering the power of repeated images.

Turning 29, again!

Home away from Home

we've moved!

Kitch

project . . .
Faux Die-cut Cards

Instructions:

1. Measure card width. Measure to that dimension from bottom front of card along length and mark on both sides.

2. Open card. Cut off top front at marks, making bottom front square. Apply floral stickers onto extended top of inside.

3. Trim around top edge of floral stickers, creating faux die-cut edge.

4. Cut green paper to size of card front.. Adhere paper onto card front.

5. Cut blue cardstock into square 1" smaller than paper.

6. Center and adhere onto green paper.

7. Cut white cardstock into square ¼" smaller than blue.

8. Write message on white cardstock. Center and adhere message onto blue cardstock.

9. Apply border onto bottom of white square.

Materials

Cardstocks: dark blue; white
Coordinating floral and border stickers
Green leaf-printed paper
Paper adhesive
Rectangular card

Tools

Craft scissors
Paper cutter
Pen
Ruler

The cards pictured at right use stickers to transform one edge of the card into a faux die-cut edge:

On the rectangular card, the sticker is placed at the bottom edge of the card. The portion of the card that would have appeared beneath the sticker has been cut away, following the lines of the sticker, creating a faux die-cut edge. A contrasting sticker peeks out from the card's interior, highlighting the cut edge.

On the photograph card, the flower is applied onto the inside edge of the frame, breaking the natural oval line. The ends of the border sticker that lies beneath the frame have been cut in a traditional "V" cut, also known as a rattail cut, making it look like ribbon.

—————design tips—————→

A die-cut is an item (usually paper but occasionally fabric, wood, metal, or plastic) cut with a die-cutting tool into a specific shape. Stickers are usually cut into the shape of whatever they represent; for example, a tulip sticker is cut into a tulip shape. These shapes are fun to emphasize by placing them so that they are partially offset on the edge of a card or scrapbook page. Use the instructions on page 76 to make the square anniversary card below.

project . . .
Reinforcements Picture Frame

Instructions:

1. Cut colored paper 1" larger all around than cardboard frame, and black cardstock slightly smaller than frame.

2. Center and adhere paper onto frame. Place paper side down on cutting board.

3. Draw "x" in frame window from corner to corner. Using craft knife, cut along "x".

4. Fold and adhere triangular shapes onto back of frame. Using burnishing tool, make certain paper lies completely flat on both front and back of frame.

5. Center and cut opening in black square slightly larger than frame opening.

6. Apply hole reinforcements onto black cardstock in random pattern. Make certain pattern extends off edges of cardstock.

7. Using craft knife, trim off any excess reinforcements that hang over edge.

8. Center and adhere black square onto frame front.

9. Adhere photograph onto back of frame. Using white craft glue, adhere backing onto back of frame. Clamp pieces together until glue sets.

Materials

Black cardstock
Colored paper
Paper adhesive
Square cardboard frame and backing
White craft glue
White hole reinforcements

Tools

Burnishing tool
Craft knife
Cutting board
Paper clamps
Paper cutter
Pencil

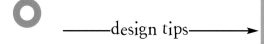

——design tips——→

White stickers can be custom colored as desired.

Create a liner for the inside of a cylindrical vase. Place a smaller vase inside to hold water and flowers.

Create silly faces by cutting into the circle stickers to create the features.

Show children how to overlap circle stickers on paper to create imaginative bugs.

While not intended for the creative paper artist, inexpensive office supply stickers can provide a springboard for the imagination. Generally, stickers found in office supply stores fall into three categories: circles, available in limited colors, white, yellow, lime green, and orange; rectangles, available in the same colors; and donut-shaped reinforcements. This attention-grabbing picture frame is simple enough to make in an hour, yet has terrific graphic appeal. Best of all, it can be made for pennies.

project . . .
Dressing Up Hearts

Do you have a basic black dress in your closet? Something simple to which you can add an accessory and change the look of it? Take a look in your sticker closet. I'll bet you have a "basic" in there, too—something that can be dressed up in different ways for different occasions. On these pages, simple heart stickers are the launching pad, but notice how unique each one looks!

Heart Tag

Set the stage for an important message by layering a sticker phrase onto a heart.

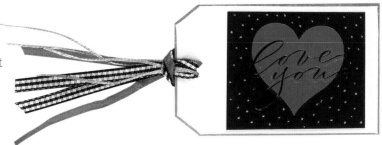

Lace Heart

A plain purple heart is layered with lace stickers to create an antique look.

Heart Frame

Frame it! A heart can be a perfect blank canvas to showcase smaller stickers, like these charming flowers. Add scalloped-paper layering behind it that has been punched with a micro punch and you have a delightful valentine.

Striped Heart

Can a tiger change its stripes? Who knows?! But a sticker surely can. Stripes are layered evenly across this heart on the diagonal, giving it a lot of graphic punch.

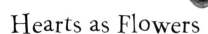

Hearts as Flowers

A heart image need not be used literally. Turn them into flowers by adding thin border stickers for the stems and a small piece of border sticker trimmed into a simple leaf shape.

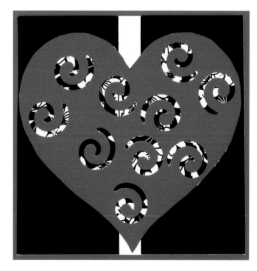

Punched Heart

Get out your decorative punches and really jazz up a heart! Here, it is punched with a swirl and then layered with black-and-white paper.

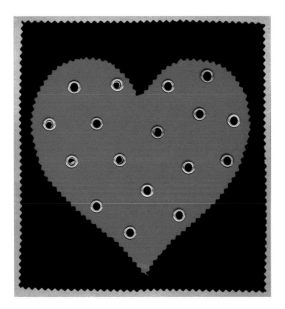

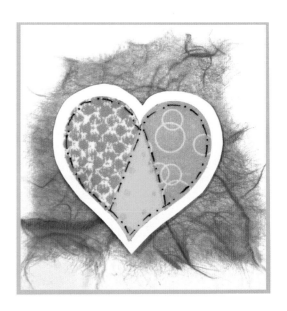

Grommet Heart

Insert grommets throughout the heart to add texture and visual interest. Create a new edge to the heart by trimming it with decorative scissors.

Tri-color Heart

Pink, yellow, blue? Why decide? Create a sticker with all three colors. Simply cut out each sticker close to its border while it is still on the release paper. Stack them together and cut through all three stickers at the same time. Reassemble them, using one piece from each sticker. Embellish your new pieced sticker with small stitch lines, drawn with a fine-point pen.

Heart Charms

Simply charming! To use hearts as charms, punch tiny holes in them and threading them onto a gold cord. Attach foam tape onto the back of the hearts to secure them to the card.

Open Heart

This heart has flipped its lid. Simply slice off the top of the heart and reposition it so that it appears to be pried open. Add stickers of any theme to "float" out of the heart. Here, musical notes emerge, but flowers, candy, or phrases would work just as well.

Multiple Hearts

Magnificent multiples. Clustering several hearts together creates a new single image that is very eye-catching.

Embossed Heart

Add texture to stickers by using them with dry embossing templates. Apply the sticker to paper and use a light-box and stylus to impress the template pattern into it.

83

project . . .
We've Moved Card

When you have interesting dimensional stickers, they pack a lot more design punch when they are repeated. They lend a nice rhythm to the page and draw attention to the details of the stickers.

Instructions:

1. Tear three rectangles approximately 1¾" × 3¼" from construction paper into.

2. Adhere rectangles onto cardstock as shown in photograph.

3. Tear strip approximately 7" × ¾" from construction paper.

4. Adhere strip onto bottom of cardstock.

5. Apply one house each onto right and left rectangles.

6. Draw line between houses, across center rectangle.

7. Write message on strip with black marker.

8. Glue buttons onto tan paper as desired.

Materials

Blue cardstock, 7" × 5"
Buttons
Paper adhesive
Tan construction paper
Three-dimensional house stickers (2)
White craft glue

Tools

Black marker
Ruler

 design tip

Repeating an image also can be used to tell a small story or add a bit of narrative interest. Try portraying a special present like this: Begin with a dog's eyes and the top of his head peaking out of an opened gift box. With each repetition let the dog become more visible until the present is fully revealed. Bare feet trekking across a page, different positions of a leaf drifting down, and a bug flying in loop-di-loop add motion to any card. As you look at your stickers, think about the impact they could have if they were repeated.

Trip to Japan Scrapbook Page

Creating a scrapbook page that is unified, has impact, and keeps the focus on the photographs need not be difficult to achieve. Several elements as shown here work together to create a truly beautiful and focused page.

The color palette is limited to warm earth tones, chosen to coordinate with the photograph's colors; the dimensional stickers are repeated, adding rhythm and interest; and the background paper is quietly stunning with several colors of ivory and cream sewn together. You can't help but look at the photographs, and appreciate the entire page.

Turning 29, Again Scrapbook Page

Remember playing dress-up when you were little? Now you can play dress-up with stickers! Many stickers are designed for use with photographs. They add a whimsical, often humorous touch and they are great at helping set the mood of a page. Try bunny ears and nose on Grandpa in Easter shots, a Santa hat on your cat, or simply crop the head from a photograph and place it on a sticker figure.

The journaling card on this page resembles a birthday card. The decorative cover opens to reveal a journaling card. To allow the card to open, two ¾" x 4" tabs were folded in half and adhered half onto the inside of the card's front and half onto the page. The tabs on the page are covered by the card's back piece.

Unconventional Use of Stickers

Why keep your stickers exculsively for your scrapbooks and cards? Let them brighten up all types of projects for all occasions. This chapter will give you some ideas for places where you can put your stickers to work: laminated onto a tote bag, garnishment for your picnic table, embellishing decorations for a birthday party, introducing a new baby, bedecking ornaments for your Christmas tree; adorning a bookmark in a book, embellishing the cover of a favorite album.

WOOF!

peek a boo

project . . .
Glass Ornaments

At holiday time, everyone looks for a pretty, useful gift idea that can be made quickly and inexpensively. Look no further. Here, stickers and decorative paper are layered under flat glass ornaments to create a lovely keepsake. Best of all, they can be made in about ten minutes and for under a dollar each!

Instructions:

1. Trace ornament shape onto decorative paper and cut out.

2. Center and apply sticker onto cutout.

3. Brush decoupage medium onto one side of glass ornament. Place cutout, image side down, onto medium.

4. Using hand, smooth out air bubbles. Let dry completely.

5. Paint edges of ornament with gold paint pen.

6. Using pencil, poke a small hole through paper covering glass ornament's hole and tie on gold cord.

Materials

Christmas stickers
Decorative paper
Decoupage medium
Flat glass Christmas ornament
Gold cord

Tools

Craft scissors
Foam brush
Gold paint pen
Pencil

—— design tips ——▶

Applying a sticker to the underside of a glass plate creates a perfect addition to a holiday table.

Create earrings by mounting small stickers onto the backs of tiny glass squares. Solder earring hooks or jump rings onto the backs.

project . . .
Pooch Gift Bag

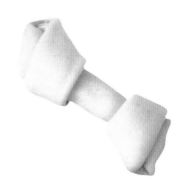

This handy tote bag always produces a smile and is simple to make. Use photographic stickers of your favorite mutt, or include snapshots of your own furry friend.

Instructions:

1. Cut paper to desired dimensions of bag.

Note: In the bag pictured here, the front and back panels measure 6½" x 8", the sides measure 3¼" x 8" , and the bottom measures 6½" x 3¼".

2. Apply dog stickers onto tote's front, back, and sides. Encase each piece, including bottom, with laminating sheets.

3. Measure and mark each tote piece for holes along sides and bottom. Be certain holes line up evenly.

4. Using ⅛" hole punch, punch holes at marks. Center and punch one hole at top of front and back pieces.

5. Set eyelets in each hole.

6. Tie front, back, and sides onto bottom with small pieces of ribbon, making certain ribbon ends remain on inside of bag. Then work your way up the sides. Trim off excess ribbon.

Note: As you tie sides together, don't tie ribbons too tightly. Sides need to "give" a little so bag hangs properly.

Materials

⅛"-wide black satin ribbon
¼" plastic tubing (1 yard)
Dog-bone print papers (2)
Dog stickers (3 sheets)
Self-adhesive laminating sheets (6)

Tools

Craft scissors
Eyelet setter
Hammer
Hole punches: ⅛"; ¼"
Pencil
Ruler

7. Using ¼" hole punch, punch one evenly spaced hole between center eyelet and each outside edge along tops of front and back.

8. Cut tubing in half and thread tubing ends into holes from outside to inside for handles.

9. Knot tubing ends to secure and trim off excess.

10. Tie small pieces of ribbon in all holes along top of tote.

Make a small version of this tote and fill it with candy, small soaps, or a bag of potpourri for a party favor.

Need a unique centerpiece idea? Using stickers and paper that coordinate with the theme of your party, create the tote without the handles as a container for a vase of flowers or a potted plant.

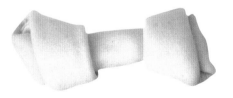

———design tips———>

project . . .
Lavender Photo Album

Instructions for tag:

1. Using marker, draw small dots and write message on tag.

2. Apply borders and small flowers onto tag.

3. Tie ribbon onto tag.

Materials

Craft glue
Decorative papers: purple striped; yellow
Lavender fabric-covered photo album
Paper adhesive
Purple gingham ribbon
Stickers: floral borders; small flowers
White tag

Tools

Green fine-tipped marker
Ruler

Instructions for cover:

1. Measure width and height of front cover.

2. Tear yellow paper 2" smaller than album width and 2" longer than height.

3. Center and glue paper onto center of front cover. Glue excess paper at top and bottom over edge of album and onto inside.

4. Tear purple-striped paper slightly narrower than yellow paper, but just as long. Center and glue onto yellow paper.

5. Glue tag onto center of album.

6. Fluff ribbon so it appears to cascade across top of album. Glue each ribbon tail into place.

7. Cut border sticker 2" longer than height of front cover and apply onto each side, securing excess sticker at top and bottom onto inside.

8. Cut purple-striped paper slightly smaller than dimensions of front cover.

9. Glue to inside of front cover, hiding raw edges of papers and sticker.

— design tip —→

To make certain the sticker will stick to your fabric cover, test a sticker on an extra piece of the fabric choice before beginning the project.

Decorating a fabric photo album with stickers is a great idea for a different look. Stickers won't produce the same kind of strong bond on fabrics that they will on paper, so avoid any fabrics with a heavy texture, pile, nap, or embossed pattern. Cotton, silk, and linen work very well. If your project will be gently used, as in the case of this photo album, stickers should hold up and are a terrific choice for decorating an album cover.

project . . .
Ice Bucket Insert

Instructions:

Note: The bucket insert is not an exact rectangle. It is rectangular in shape with a slight arc to it. This allows the liner to sit evenly inside ice bucket.

1. Remove plastic liner and decorative plastic insert from ice bucket.

2. Tape two pieces of white cardstock together at short ends. Trace decorative plastic insert onto white cardstock and cut out.

3. Adhere vellum onto cardstock. Trim away excess vellum.

Note: You will need to abut pieces of vellum so there is no overlap and no gap.

4. Cut thin border strips from one scrapbook paper and adhere onto top and bottom of vellum-covered cardstock. Cut five small rectangles from coordinating papers. Evenly space and adhere onto vellum.

5. Apply floral stickers onto centers of rectangles.

6. Insert decorated cardstock into ice bucket and replace plastic liner.

Materials

11" × 14" white cardstock (2)
Assorted coordinating scrapbook papers
Assorted floral stickers
Cellophane tape
Ice bucket with removable plastic liner
Paper adhesive
Vellum
Vellum adhesive

Tools

Craft scissors
Paper cutter

———design tips———→

You can also make napkin rings to complete the patio set in the photograph. To make napkin rings, simply loop a strip of scrapbook paper and glue edges together. Apply a sticker onto the paper, or make it sturdier by attaching the sticker onto cardstock and cutting out before attaching onto paper.

Patio Set

Creating a customized look for a party is easy and inexpensive with stickers. Here, an ice bucket liner and napkin ring are transformed with pretty papers and coordinating stickers. Place mats and place cards are natural additions.

project . . .
Party Hat

Create your own party hats from paper plates or purchase one-color hats from a party store. Dress them up with stickers and include the fun ribbon spray on top of the hat.

Instructions:

1. Trace circumference of paper plate onto cardstock. Cut out circle.

2. Mark center of circle. Using ruler, draw line through center of circle and cut into equal halves.

3. Pull corners together and glue or staple together for hat.

4. Punch holes on each side of hat. Secure one end of elastic into each hole.

5. Decorate hat with stickers to portray appropriate theme.

6. Attach ribbon spray onto top of hat and secure with craft glue.

Materials

12" paper plate
Cardstock
Ribbon spray
Stickers that match theme
Thin elastic string

Tools

Craft scissors
Hole punch
Pencil
Ruler
White craft glue or stapler

Jungle-themed Birthday Party

"Party Animals" is the theme depicted here. The three elements working together that kick this party into high gear are the colors: red, purple, and yellow; theme: animals and colorful polka dots dress up everything from napkin rings to gift bags; and the accents: black-and-white stripes on the zebra and the checkered border provide a graphic punch.

project . . .
Place mat

If you need a simple activity to keep little guests busy during the party, let them make their own place mats before you serve the cake.

Materials

Cardstocks or construction papers:
purple; red; yellow

Self-adhesive laminating sheets or clear contact paper

Stickers: jungle-themed; lettering

Tools

Crayons or markers (optional)
Paper cutter

Instructions:

1. Using paper cutter, cut cardstock or construction paper to desired size for place mat.

Note: Complete this step before the party begins or purchase paper that is already the correct size.

2. Apply stickers onto paper.

Note: You can also use crayons or markers to write a name onto the mat.

3. When design is completed, apply laminating sheets or contact paper onto both sides of mat.

Baby Boy's First Birthday

In this ensemble, the highlights of a baby boy's first year of life are neatly tied together. Again the color, theme, and accents combine to tie the projects together.

project . . . Invitation

Although handmade invitations take more effort than the store-bought variety, they are always a welcome treat. This invitation was made to match the theme of the party.

Instructions:

1. Cut border sticker to width of card and apply along card bottom.

2. Cut vellum to desired size.

3. Stamp party stamp onto card and date, time, and place stamps onto vellum.

4. Attach vellum onto card by setting eyelets in diagonal corners.

5. Apply duck and carriage stickers onto cardstock and cut out.

6. Attach cutouts onto invitation with foam tape.

Note: A tiny duck sticker is tucked into the baby carriage for a bit of whimsy.

Materials

Cardstock
Decorative eyelets
Foam tape
Rectangular card
Stickers: baby carriage; decorative border; ducks, Vellum

Tools

Blue ink pad
Craft scissors
Eyelet setter
Hammer
Hole punch
Paper cutter
Rubber stamps: date; time; party; place

Materials

Cardstock

Decorative eyelets

Decorative fibers

Decorative tag

Foam tape

Paper adhesive

Photograph

Scrapbook papers with coordinating designs (2)

Stickers: duck; letters; rope border; sailboat; star; other assorted as desired.

Tools

Eyelet setter

Hammer

Hole punch

To keep this page matching the theme of the party, decorative eyelets set over stickers embellish the corners. A small piece of the rope border sticker creates a wave effect for the toy boat to "sail" on.

Instructions:

1. Adhere one piece of paper onto cardstock.

2. Fold second paper in half along diagonal. Adhere outside edges onto first paper, creating a pocket on diagonal.

3. Set eyelets into three corners of folded page.

4. Apply sailboat sticker onto cardstock and cut out.

5. Attach cutout onto page with foam tape.

6. Apply rope border onto page under sail boat, creating wave.

7. Tie tag onto page with decorative fibers.

8. Apply other stickers as desired.

project . . .
Acrylic Bookmark

Several sticker companies make "mirror image" stickers, that is, the same image but facing the opposite direction. These stickers offer a wonderful opportunity to use them back to back, because they line up perfectly. This acrylic bookmark—a terrific gift idea—features images on both sides, creating "ooohs" from the grateful recipient.

Instructions:

1. Apply single images onto acrylic tag.

2. Flip tag over and apply mirror images directly over counterparts.

3. Tie on ribbons.

Materials

Acrylic tag
Decorative ribbons
Stickers with mirror images

Stickers on Mirrors

Use ready-made stickers to embellish a mirror, or create your own by drawing, painting, or photocopying and enlarging art onto white adhesive-backed paper. Here, stickers were layered on top of each other to create the complete scene.

Stencils

Here's a riddle: When can you see a sticker that is not there? When it is used as a stencil, of course. Stickers come in a huge variety of shapes, which make them perfect elements to use as stencils. This chapter will show you how to create sticker stencils and use them with paints—brush-on and spray, inks, and embossing powders.

Simply place the sticker on a nonpourous surface, apply the paint, ink, or embossing powder, then remove the sticker while these coverings are still a little bit wet. When using stickers as stencils on pourous surfaces, re-move some of the adhesive backing first by pouncing the sticker up and down several times on a piece of fabric—this will make it easier to remove.

project . . .
Star Votive Holders

Votive candles are great mood setters for any room. Using star-shaped stickers as stencils, create votive holders that add twinkling evening light to your table.

Materials

Frosted-glass spray: blue; white
Glass votive holders (2)
Star stickers

Tool

Craft knife (optional)

Instructions:

1. Spray votive holders with frosted white paint. Let dry for one hour.

2. Apply star stickers onto votive holders.

3. Spray votive holders with frosted blue paint. Let dry for one hour.

4. Using fingernails or tip of craft knife, remove stars.

Materials

Ceramic paints: assorted colors; black
Circle stickers
Unglazed oval platter

Tools

Burnishing tool
Craft knife
Kiln
Paintbrushes: fine-tipped; medium
Sponge

project . . .
Polka-dot Tray

Paint-your-own pottery studios are popular in many towns and cities. They allow anyone to create decorative, durable, and safe-to-use serving and accent pieces. By using stickers as stencils on "greenware"—the technical term for pottery before it has been glazed and fired—crafters can create interesting patterns and shapes.

Instructions:

1. Rinse platter thoroughly with water to remove dust. Let air-dry for several minutes.

2. Apply stickers onto inside of platter. Burnish sticker edges with finger or burnishing tool.

3. Using medium paintbrush, apply black paint over platter top. Let air dry for several minutes.

4. Using tip of craft knife, remove stickers.

5. Using fine-tipped paintbrush, apply dot of colorful paint inside each circle.

6. Lightly sponge black paint onto outside of platter base.

7. Have studio fire piece.

project . . .
Storybook Caddy

Instructions:

1. Apply tape over nameplate to protect it from paint. Using foam brush, paint magazine caddy with gesso. Let dry for 30 minutes.

Note: Gesso is used as a base coat to seal, smooth, and tint the surface being prepped for paint. Paint adheres to gesso very well. Oftentimes, an additional coat of paint is not necessary if a surface has been prepped with gesso.

2. Using second foam brush, paint caddy with two coats of white paint. Let dry at least 30 minutes between each coat.

3. Form words with alphabet stickers and apply stickers onto caddy.

Note: Allow words to wrap around corners of caddy. Vary the placement and types of stickers used. Burnish all the edges down with your finger or an old credit card.

4. Sponge outside of caddy with pink, avoiding raised edge. Let dry for several minutes.

5. Using craft knife, remove stickers.

Note: It is easier to remove stickers while everything is slightly damp.

6. Apply border sticker onto center of raised edge. Miter corners as described on page 64.

7. Let caddy dry for several hours.

Materials

Cardboard magazine caddy with nameplate

Cellophane tape

Gesso

Glossy decoupage medium

Paints: white; pink

Stickers: alphabet stickers in assorted sizes and fonts (5 sets); pink checkered borders

Tools

Craft knife

Craft scissors

Cutting board

Foam brushes (3)

Round cosmetic sponge (or any sponge with small holes)

Small paintbrush

8. Using clean foam brush, apply decoupage medium onto pink areas. Let dry for one hour before handling.

Note: This will help protect the surface of the caddy and give it a nice shine.

9. Remove tape from nameplate.

Gather a variety of your alphabet stickers and create this charming caddy to hold bedtime stories.

project . . .
Chinese Lantern

Instructions:

1. Assemble lantern frame according to package directions.

2. Paint frame with two coats of black. Let dry completely between coats.

3. Varnish frame according to manufacturer's directions. Let dry completely.

4. Cut four panels from vellum to fit lantern sides.

5. Trace one sticker on scratch paper. Cut out image, leaving approximately ½" border all around for mask.

6. Apply fan stickers onto centers of vellum panels.

7. Tear strips of mulberry paper and adhere onto vellum edges with glue stick.

8. On back of vellum panel, hold mask over sticker image. Stamp back panel. Remove mask. Sprinkle on embossing powder. Tap off excess, then heat-emboss image.

9. Attach panels to inside of frame with double-sided tape.

Materials

Black paint
Clear cement
Clear embossing ink
Color-coordinated beads
Double-sided tape
Fan stickers
Lantern kit
Heavy-weight vellum
Mulberry paper with chinese lettering
Scrap paper
Spray-on varnish
Straight pins (4)
White/glitter embossing powder

Tools

Craft scissors
Double-sided tape
Embossing gun
Glue stick
Paintbrush
Paper cutter
Pencil
Texture stamp
Wire cutters

10. Thread beads onto each pin. Place a dot of cement in between the beads and press together. Cement top of pin onto each frame corner. Using wire cutters, remove excess pin. Let dry completely.

11. Screw in lightbulb.

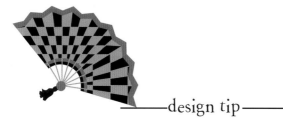

—design tip——→

Give the panels added interest by stamping around the sticker with a texture stamp and embossing with sparkling embossing powder.

"Guang Hui" is the Chinese word for radiant light.
You can create this lovely source of radiant light by
using a lantern kit, decorative papers, and stickers.

Stickers Made from Unusual Materials

Probably the most exciting innovation in the sticker world has been the introduction of "non-paper" stickers. Today stickers are made from metal, plastic, fabric, leather, and acetate, just to name a few. This chapter will show you some ideas for ways to incorporate these stickers made from novel materials into projects that showcase them to their fullest advantage and hopefully inspire you to begin to work with them, too.

project . . . Altered Book

Instructions:

1. Mix small amount of each color paint with equal parts of glazing medium. Brush paint mixture onto pages of book. Use your fingers to swirl paint together in places. Let paint dry for one hour.

Note: The effect should be a continuous wash of color that fades in and out from salmon to goldenrod.

2. Cut out copied vintage images and adhere onto decorative paper. Trim paper with decorative scissors. Add small stitch marks with pen.

3. Trim copied recipes with decorative scissors.

4. Apply chalks with fingers to give recipe an aged appearance.

5. On right-hand side of book, adhere about six pages together.

Note: Depending on the thickness of the page and the depth of your buttons, you may need to glue more pages together to create a window of adequate depth.

6. Once dried, place cutting board underneath stack of glued pages. Using pencil, draw window where desired. Using craft knife, cut out window.

Note: You may need to cut through the page layers several times to fully remove the window.

7. Place window cutout on decorative paper and trace around it. Cut out window shape, then cut out window center ⅛" smaller all around than traced lines.

Materials

Acrylic paints: salmon; goldenrod
Clay buttons (2)
Chalks: red; yellow
Cookbook
Decorative papers
Glazing medium
Red dye ink
Paper adhesive
Stickers: border; flat-backed marbles with lettering
Vintage recipes and art from cookbooks (color-copied and enlarged or reduced, as necessary)

Tools

Black pen
Craft knife
Cutting board
Decorative scissors
Paintbrush
Pencil
Small rubber stamp

Note: By creating a frame in which the cut-out window is slightly smaller than actual window, any messy cut marks will be disguised.

8. Draw in small stitch marks with pen.

9. Layer small piece of decorative paper underneath window so it "peaks" through. Adhere two strips of decorative paper along right- and left-hand page edges.

10. Adhere decorative paper squares and window frame onto page. Glue two buttons inside window.

11. Apply border sticker around entire diameter of open pages. Apply lettering stickers onto page. Using red ink, stamp image randomly around page.

Altering books is a new and exciting art form that is attracting artists and crafters alike. Rather than beginning a project or a journal with blank white paper, altered-book artists choose to begin their work on the pages of a book. Using obsolete books is a great way to recycle books you no longer use. One idea is to choose a book that has a cover you really like.

An altered book can take any form the artist likes. Creating pop-up, pocket, and torn pages; cutting windows and niches; and applying paints, chalks, and rubber-stamping are just the beginning of the possibilities. These books often include three-dimensional objects like the clear pebble letter stickers shown here, to entice the viewer to touch as well as look.

project . . .
Metal Tag Journal

Metal stickers make the perfect focal point for a small box, card, or journal. Although the stickers come without color, it is simple to add color with permanent markers to virtually bring out the detail.

Instructions:

1. Cut paper slightly smaller than dimensions of journal cover. Adhere onto inside of front cover.

2. Color metal sticker with permanent markers as desired.

3. Center and apply metal sticker onto paper in window.

4. Apply frame stickers onto front cover, framing window. Apply corner stickers onto cover corners.

5. Cut ribbon 6" longer than journal height. Tape bottom 3" of ribbon onto upper right-hand corner of inside cover for bookmark.

6. Color metal mirror-image stickers as desired.

7. Apply mirror images onto remaining end of bookmark.

Materials

Cellophane tape
Green paper
Journal with window cut into cover
Paper adhesive
Ribbon
Stickers: frames; decorative corners; metal with mirror image

Tools

Craft scissors
Permanent markers
Ruler

——— design tips ———→

Consider using metal stickers on picture frames, decorative boxes, or decorative pots or planters.

Insert a ribbon loop in between two metal stickers for a quick and easy ornament idea.

project . . .
Folded Booklet Card

Instructions for card:

1. Using colored pencils, color sticky side of sticker. Apply sticker onto foil and trim off excess foil.

2. Adhere sticker, foil side down, onto folded purple cardstock ⅛" from fold. Trim card edges ⅛" larger than sticker.

3. Cut ribbon in half. Center and glue one end of first ribbon onto right-hand edge inside of card.

4. Cut 1" strip from patterned paper. Glue strip along right-hand edge over ribbon end on inside of card. Trim edges of strip even with card.

5. Accordion-fold paper to fit inside card. Glue one side of paper onto inside card back.

Note: In the card pictured on page 121, a patterned paper flourish was glued over the edge of the folded paper that has been glued onto the inside of the card.

6. Center and glue second ribbon end onto right-hand edge on back of card.

7. Adhere cardstocks and decorative papers in graduated layers as desired for card mat.

Note: Here, corners were cut from decorative papers and adhered onto corners of paper.

8. Glue card onto mat.

Materials

Acetate floral sticker
Cardstocks: gold; sage green; purple sparkle (2)
Craft glue
Decorative papers: celery green; patterned green (2)
Ivory paper (12")
Organza ribbon (18")
Paper adhesive
Silver leaf charm

Tools

Colored pencils
Craft scissors
Hole punches: round; square
Paper cutter

Instructions for folder:

1. Fold purple cardstock in half so folded size is approximately ½" larger than card for folder. Glue short edges together.

2. Using round hole punch, punch portion of circle for use as a finger tab to remove card.

3. Using square punch, punch squares from purple and gold cardstocks. Angle and glue onto front of folder in a layered pattern.

4. Center and glue charm onto squares.

The cards featured below and on page 122 are made with unique stickers—the images are all detailed line-art printed on adhesive-backed clear acetate.

In the small booklet card below, colored pencils were applied to the sticky side of the sticker before it was adhered onto the paper.

A variety of backgrounds can be added and, because of the clear acetate, the backgrounds will radically change the look of the sticker. They allow the artist to supply the background, creating a completely customized look.

Flapper Girl Card

Once again using the clear acetate sticker, this Flapper Girl Card makes a beautiful gift card or can be used as a decorative piece. Here, gold foil was applied to the back of the sticker; but chalks, glitters, and pearlescent powders are also options. A small slice at the top of the head allows a feather to slide behind. Tiny dots of glue were applied with a toothpick around the neck to create a necklace.

The Elk's Annual

EGG HUNT

This was Valynn's very first Egg Hunt with the public. We were not ready for the fight for eggs! She only got two! The whole event was over with in seconds. But we had lots of fun!

Easter Page

This charming Easter page is a feast for the eyes as well as the touch because of the inclusion of embroidered patch stickers. The felt flowers embellished with sequins, the embroidered butterfly, and the die-cut embroidered flowers in the bunny's basket, all add texture and visual appeal. They are a snap to apply onto any surface simply by removing the release paper and pressing them into place, just like you would any sticker.

Metric Equivalency Chart

Inches to Millimetres and Centimetres

inches	mm	cm	inches	cm	inches	cm
⅛	3	0.3	9	22.9	30	76.2
¼	6	0.6	10	25.4	31	78.7
½	13	1.3	12	30.5	33	83.8
⅝	16	1.6	13	33.0	34	86.4
¾	19	1.9	14	35.6	35	88.9
⅞	22	2.2	15	38.1	36	91.4
1	25	2.5	16	40.6	37	94.0
1 ¼	32	3.2	17	43.2	38	96.5
1 ½	38	3.8	18	45.7	39	99.1
1 ¾	44	4.4	19	48.3	40	101.6
2	51	5.1	20	50.8	41	104.1
2 ½	64	6.4	21	53.3	42	106.7
3	76	7.6	22	55.9	43	109.2
3 ½	89	8.9	23	58.4	44	111.8
4	102	10.2	24	61.0	45	114.3
4 ½	114	11.4	25	63.5	46	116.8
5	127	12.7	26	66.0	47	119.4
6	152	15.2	27	68.6	48	121.9
7	178	17.8	28	71.1	49	124.5
8	203	20.3	29	73.7	50	127.0

Yards to Metres

yards	metres	yards	metres	yards	metres	yards	metres	yards	metres
⅛	0.11	2 ⅛	1.94	4 ⅛	3.77	6 ⅛	5.60	8 ⅛	7.43
¼	0.23	2 ¼	2.06	4 ¼	3.89	6 ¼	5.72	8 ¼	7.54
⅜	0.34	2 ⅜	2.17	4 ⅜	4.00	6 ⅜	5.83	8 ⅜	7.66
½	0.46	2 ½	2.29	4 ½	4.11	6 ½	5.94	8 ½	7.77
⅝	0.57	2 ⅝	2.40	4 ⅝	4.23	6 ⅝	6.06	8 ⅝	7.89
¾	0.69	2 ¾	2.51	4 ¾	4.34	6 ¾	6.17	8 ¾	8.00
⅞	0.80	2 ⅞	2.63	4 ⅞	4.46	6 ⅞	6.29	8 ⅞	8.12
1	0.91	3	2.74	5	4.57	7	6.40	9	8.23
1 ⅛	1.03	3 ⅛	2.86	5 ⅛	4.69	7 ⅛	6.52	9 ⅛	8.34
1 ¼	1.14	3 ¼	2.97	5 ¼	4.80	7 ¼	6.63	9 ¼	8.46
1 ⅜	1.26	3 ⅜	3.09	5 ⅜	4.91	7 ⅜	6.74	9 ⅜	8.57
1 ½	1.37	3 ½	3.20	5 ½	5.03	7 ½	6.86	9 ½	8.69
1 ⅝	1.49	3 ⅝	3.31	5 ⅝	5.14	7 ⅝	6.97	9 ⅝	8.80
1 ¾	1.60	3 ¾	3.43	5 ¾	5.26	7 ¾	7.09	9 ¾	8.92
1 ⅞	1.71	3 ⅞	3.54	5 ⅞	5.37	7 ⅞	7.20	9 ⅞	9.03
2	1.83	4	3.66	6	5.49	8	7.32	10	9.14

Acknowledgments

The author and publisher would like to thank the following artists for their contributions to the book:

Kelly Carolla for Mrs. Grossman's Paper Co., pages 39, 45, 98–100
Veronik Caron, page 55
Dee Gruenig, pages 12, 104
Paige Hill, pages 14–15, 24–25, 34–35, 48–49, 58–59, 74–75, 88–89, 106–107, 114–115

Rob Reynolds, photographs, page 73
Lysa Schwartz, page 122
Marie-Eve Trudeau, page 51
Annette Watkins, pages 101–103
Agi Werner, pages 121–122

The following manufacturer's products were used in the projects and on the pages featured in the book:

Anna Griffin Designs
(888) 817-8170
www.annagriffin.com
pages 15, 18–21, 23

Bo-Bunny Press
(801) 771-4010
www.bobunny.com
pages 16, 42–43, 49, 52–53, 75, 90–91

Brenda Walton for K&Co.
(877) 632-7467
www.creativityshop.com
pages 58, 68–70

Bryce and Madeline from
Creative Imaginations
(800) 942-6487
www.cigift.com
pages 59, 71

Creative Imaginations
(800) 942-6487
www.cigift.com
pages 27, 111

Doodlebug Designs
(801) 524-0050
www.doodlebugdesigninc.com
page 87

The Gifted Line
(800) 5-GIFTED
pages 15, 23

Krylon
(800) 457-9566
www.krylon.com
pages 91, 108

Lasting Impressions
(801) 298-1979
www.lastingimpressions.com
pages 27, 47

Magenta
(450) 922-5253
www.magentastyle.com
pages 18, 48, 50–51, 54–55, 62–65, 72, 114–115, 118–119

Making Memories
(801) 294-0430
www.makingmemories.com
pages 15, 34, 48, 59, 74, 77, 87–88, 95, 116–117

Me and My Big Ideas
www.meandmybigideas.com
pages 75, 106–107, 112, 116

Mrs. Grossman's Paper Co.
(800) 429-4549
www.mrsgrossmans.com
pages 14, 20, 27, 32–35, 38–41, 44–45, 56–57, 61, 63, 68, 75, 80–83, 85, 87, 89, 98–100, 104, 110, 112–113, 124, 126

NRN Designs
Fax: (714) 898-0015
www.nrndesigns.com
pages 21, 59, 73, 93, 111

Paper Bliss by Westrim
(800) 727-2727
www.westrimcrafts.com
pages 84–87

Paper House Productions
(800) 255-7316
www.paperhouseproductions.com
pages 59–61, 89, 92–93

Paper Parachute
(503) 533-4513
www.paperparachute.com
pages 120–122

Posh Impressions for Mrs. Grossman's
Paper Company
(800) 429-4549
www.poshimpressions.com
pages 11, 104

Printworks Collection
(800) 854-6558
www.printworkscollection.com
pages 26–27, 35, 46–47, 88–89, 94–95, 101–103

Provo Craft
(800) 937-7686
www.provocraft.com
pages 41, 60, 89, 111, 118

Ranger Industries
(800) 244-2211
www.rangerink.com
pages 56–57

(Continued on page 126)

(Continued from page 125)

Rollabind
(800) 438-3542
www.rollabind.com
page 33

Ruby & Begonia
(801) 334-7829
Supplied props for all photographs

Seven Gypsies
(800) 588-6707
www.sevengpsies.com
page 21

Sharon Ann Collection from
Deja Views
(800) 243-8419
www.dejaviews.com
pages 10, 22, 66–67, 74, 76–77, 88, 96–97

Sizzix
(866) 742-4447
www.sizzix.com
page 11

Sonnets from Creative Imaginations
(800) 942-6487
www.cigift.com
page 27

Susan Branch
(805) 788-4822
www.susuanbranch.com
pages 40, 107

Thermoweb
(847) 520-5200
www.thermoweb.com
page 123

Whipper Snapper Designs
(888) 229-1391
www.whippersnapperdesigns.com
pages 8, 24–26, 28–31, 34, 36–37, 125

Index

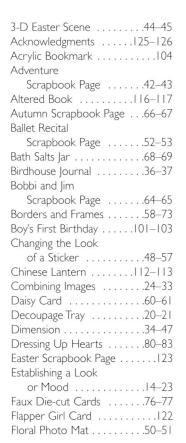

Carol Scheffler is one of the foremost authorities on Arts and Crafts in the country. She has been seen worldwide in her capacity as Arts and Crafts Contributor to NBC's Today Show. She appears regularly on CBS's Early Show in New York, in addition to many news programs around the country. She also appears regularly on DIY Asks as their craft expert, Discovery Channel, CNN, Home and Garden Television, DIY Scrapbooking, and appeared on the Rosie O'Donnell Show.

Carol is the author of four books on crafting: *Rubber Stamping for the First Time*, *Family Crafting*, *Crafting Fun Stuff with a Crowd of Kids*, and *Great Kid's Rooms*. She is proud that her books have been Book of the Month selections. She has served as craft editor for *Parents* magazine and has contributed to *Better Homes and Garden's Creative Home*, *McCall's*, and *The Rubber Stamper*.

Carol is delighted to have served as the Hobby Industry Association's spokesperson for National Craft Month. She has also been the spokesperson for the world's largest craft web site, Joann.com, and is a frequent guest expert on IVillage.com.

Carol hales from Cleveland, Ohio. She is a wife, the mother of three girls, and currently resides in a suburb of New York City.